Conscious Dying

...The Final Frontier

KAEL S. PARKER

Copyright © 2014 Kael S. Parker

All rights reserved.

All photos are mine; I took them.

ISBN: **3-00-046489-1**
ISBN-13: **978-3000464898**

DEDICATION

*To my wife, Chris,
who puts up with me every day,
and provides me with a daily
fresh breath of reality*

*"No matter where you go,
There you are."*

—Buckaroo Banzai

Where do New Yorkers go when they die?
None of your business.

Where do agnostics go?
I don't know.

"Only when you are truly conscious and aware do you begin to wake up from the dream."
—Joe Dispenza, *Breaking the Habit of Being Yourself: How to Lose Your Mind and Create a New One*

CONTENTS

	Acknowledgments	i
	Introduction	1
1	What the Books Say	7
2	What the Research Says	15
3	Smoke This	17
4	Roll Your Own	21
5	Bus Stops and Umbrellas	25
6	Body Dynamics	27
7	Intermezzo	31
8	More Body Dynamics	33
9	The Final Answer	37
10	Finis	39
	References	41

ACKNOWLEDGMENTS

To the crazy Australian Bernie Clarke,
who introduced an atheist to *I Ching* in an Amsterdam hostel.

Introduction

What this book is and isn't
The book in your hands is a workbook for the subject of...death. Do you notice a clenching in heart and stomach at the word? You can talk to that in this book.

This book is there to push your envelope. Feel free to flip around to the parts that catch your attention. It is filled with information that for many people is at the edge or outside of where they have till now filled their thoughts, or ever wanted to. But then, dying itself is a place most people put off thinking about until the last minute, and think they have never been before, can't know anything about beforehand, and may never go to again. But is it really so strange, fearsome, and unknown? Read on to find out.

This is a workbook to practice what it could be like when and after you die. It is a workbook about why you feel fear and sadness about dying, or about someone else dying. It is a workbook about things people leave undone, unsaid, or unthought before they die. In it are exercises—guided meditations—to explore different parts of yourself you might have forgotten about or put aside for later, which may rear their heads as unbidden monsters along your path in uncharted realms as you sail off the edge of the earth.

And if after all there really is nothing after death but a great precipice after which is black nothing? Well, when you read this book beforehand you can go into the nothing with a clean conscience, with messy loose ends all tied up. It's your cliff to jump over.

People who pick up this book likely have had dying appear in their world, whether it be their own or others'. Dying is a scary place for most, a place where no one goes willingly, but everyone goes someday. Yes, Jim, it is the final frontier.

Dying is the one place however where your GPS won't take you. Lots of maps supposedly exist, but they're like the treasure maps in a movie: each map only gives a part of the picture, and contradicts all the other maps until all pieces are together, or is written in a language no one understands any more.

So what good are these maps?

Not much, and a lot. They talk to a part of you you're not used to knowing is there—and the part you're used to and familiar with is annoyed or afraid to think that there are places it can't go and can't know, and dismisses places there are no maps for. But fact is fact, despite what Egyptian pharaohs thought—you really can't take anything with you when you go there. If it's physical, anyway. And that's what makes dying so scary: you leave behind you everything you ever thought was you and yours. Everything that defines you, you leave behind. And if you die and leave everything behind that defined you, what will be left that's you at all? That is the question that has fascinated me since age sixteen.

It's scary too for the people around you, in whose life you fit in different ways. For whom are you the pillar of or bane to their existence? By dying, a person changes forever the world around them, for better and worse, and that is scary for everyone involved, especially if there's little to no time to prepare for this momentous step, this last great bungee jump. So part of the function of this book is to practice preparing. Preparing for what, and how? This answer you have to find out for yourself, and if this book works right it will help you find that answer.

A word to the book title: Is there such a thing as conscious dying? When I watch some people around me, I could wonder if there is such a thing as conscious living. And some at the end of the body's life live with medications and therapies that can affect that precious clarity of mind called "consciousness", as do many pain medications for instance. Or there can be so much inner conflict and turmoil about issues and challenges still not solved and resolved and accomplished that clarity can be more a utopian Olympus than a daily companion. But the word "conscious" can mean simply the intent or desire to be aware of one's processes. So in other words you don't have to first reach the austere sublimity of the mountain monk to approach your dying—and living—in a more conscious way. You start right from where you are.

As for the terms "Conscious" and "Dying":
"Conscious" means you can remember it the next day—or try to—and "Dying" means the irreparable separation of consciousness from body. So some day you too will find out if you can remember it the next day, even after you have left your body behind.

Is there life after death? It is not the purpose of this book to answer this question for you, so get used to that up front. That's your problem to hash out. Rather, one purpose is to raise that question, hold it in one's hands and turn it around, read the label on the bottom of the vessel, sniff the contents—to take the charge out of the subject, and even to taste the contents in one's thoughts...or to remember what they taste like, so that the strange and fearful unknown can at least become less fearful. And behold, the drink becomes perchance more palatable....

I do have my own clear ideas on the subject of death, and life after death, developed over many years of thought and experience, but each person must find her/his own way; there is no other way. You can get your beliefs in a fast food restaurant chain store, or in a chic New Age food store, or in a department store off the rack ready-made, or go grubbing for them among the herbs on a snowy mountain. If they feed you, that's the main thing. They can make you fat, or thin, or just right but leave funny plaques on your teeth till they fall out. And some people say that they live only from sunshine and two glasses of water a day. I say that's cool. It would sure help my checking account to live so frugally. But I enjoy the occasional steak, and glass of wine, and even try out the salad that my wife says is so good for me.

Disclaimer: in no way am I advocating harming oneself or others. So don't try to give me responsibility for your actions. And nowhere am I suggesting or condoning taking of life, whether one's own or others'. Also: if you decide to try things like reincarnation therapy or other things I write about in this book, do yourself a favor and if possible find someone who knows what they're doing to help or accompany you. There are enough people already running around suing someone else because they spilled their own hot coffee on themselves.

This book is in part written to speak to your non-linear self; so, read it like when you read a language you don't speak very well yet: put your understanding on wide focus, and look for patterns that may fit together later to make more sense.

Oh yes: parts of this book—and I won't tell you which ones; you're all grown up now, or usually like to believe so—may best be read with tongue in cheek. That keeps the smile muscles in shape and well-perfused, which is very important when discoursing on Weighty Topics. In chapters of background information, I will not pretend to present exhaustive compendia on subjects covered; my purpose is not to exhaust you, but to entertain and inform you, and provide food for thought. So don't be miffed if here and there I take creative license with the minute details; it all has a reason. Remember, an elephant observed from the back gives a completely different impression than from the front. So turn him around too, please; the front is much more prepossessing.

One version of the universe has it that there are successive and multiple coexistent levels of truth and reality which constantly interact, so that one man's next-door neighbor is an ant hill's unpredictable and vengeful god.

Another version says that it doesn't matter what you eat, but rather how you eat it. Before you is your next ten course meal. Take your time with each course; chew well, savor, digest. Take notes on the wine that goes best with each course, and let me know.

I wish you happy eating, whether it be sunshine and happy thoughts, or Sauerbraten and cigarettes.

☙

"There are 10 life states of any life: Hell, hunger, anger, animality, rapture, humanity, learning, realization, bodhisattva and buddhahood."
(Wikipedia, <u>Afterlife</u>)

1. What the Books Say

A short history of death and dying, or how they do it in other cultures. Funerals; views of afterlife

Why do people have rituals about death and dying? For whom do they have meaning? The answer to this question depends partly on whether a person continues to be conscious after the body dies. If they do, then the rituals can have importance not only to the people left behind, but also to the person who has died. The Tibetans' Book of the Dead for instance is designed more for the person passing over than for those still firmly attached to their body, so that they will understand better what they encounter on the way. Catholics believe that they can hold masses which will help their deceased loved ones reach heaven when they have gotten stuck in between, without enough tokens for the next subway. This is a great idea, and a logical continuation of praying for heavenly intercession for the living like my family has often done for me, and in general of the thesis that one's own good intentions do have an effect in one's world.

Some people who believe that the consciousness continues believe that if you are bad this life then you may come back as an insect or other punishment befitting your sins; this could be a great scare tactic so you'll be good and better in your endless lives. Others are convinced that if you're bad you will go to hell; this may be a tactic in the same category. Others simply believe that you will continue repeating your mistakes in serial lifetimes until you get it right; that's scary too, like people who keep attracting the same type of abusive relationship until they get tired of playing that game, or learn as much as they need to to not need to repeat the mistake.

Some cultures have a lot of experience in and information about dealing with death: Hindus, Chinese, Tibetans and ancient Egyptians have been around (or used to be around in the case of the ancient Egyptians) for a long, long time. From our perspective in the United States or other concurrent cultures, these peoples have existed at least back to God's fifth birthday. What they have to say about dying can be interesting and/or instructive. Trouble is though that much of this information has to be gleaned from languages so separated from us in time and space that translating or reading the text can be a true shot in the dark—an educated guess at very most as to how close the meaning comes to what was actually intended. Even translating from one living language to another has to leave out a few shades of meaning, which I notice whenever I read a translation of German: some of the nuances ALWAYS get lost. So when I first read the Bible, or Machiavelli's *The Prince*, or Lao Tzu's *Tao te Ching*, I read several translations. Sometimes for a laugh I like to ask Google's translation of various common everyday colloquial phrases; it tends to translate the words instead of the meaning. Good luck with that if you are deciphering an ancient Egyptian joke book or death manual.

Following is a small compendium of beliefs of various cultures; its purpose is mainly to illustrate the diversity and ingenuity of human thought, rather than to be complete. Complete is reserved for idiots and perfectionists.

<u>Protestant Christianity</u>:
Here we have mostly flavors of you-die-and-go-to-heaven and come back perfect at the end of time if you believed the right things. But I don't mean "come back" as in reincarnation; that hasn't been a part of the church since it was thrown out in 553 AD,[1] which was of course the church now called the Roman

Catholic church anyway. In this worldview, you have to get it right the first time, because where your consciousness will live for the remaining billions of years the Universe has left until the next Big Bang will depend on your being good now, so you'd better be good, for goodness' sake. And even if you aren't, if you are really sorry and ask God for forgiveness, then everything will be okay and you can still save your eternal you-know-what—that is, IF you do it before you die. There's no whining around after you die asking to get into Jackpot Land then. Do not pass Go; do not collect Eternal Life.

I grew up with the images of either eternal wings, haloes, and harps, or the belly of some volcano where you live hot and dirty and exhausted with some demons with horns and pitchforks to poke you all day. I could never decide which alternative would be more of a torture though, which left me in quite a quandary.

Hell
Modern visions of what Hell must be like seem to come from references in the Bible to Sheol (Hebrew), or Hades, Gehenna, or Tartarus (all Greek). All are translated in English as Hell.[2]
Matthew 13:50 "furnace of fire...weeping and gnashing of teeth"
Mark 9:48 "where their worm does not die, and the fire is not quenched."[3]

These sound to me like threats for a physical body that after death one no longer has.

Heaven
"In fact, the Bible reveals very few concrete details about heaven, the afterlife and what happens when we die.... Perhaps our finite minds could never comprehend the realities of eternity. "[4]

It's always fascinated me in this regard that there are so few science fiction stories of utopias that are actually better than what we already have, and furthermore also *workable*; most are much worse. My take is that humans can't envision a viable superior condition they haven't already experienced.

Catholic Christianity:
Here an interesting variation to the above theme comes in: when you die you first land in Purgatory,[5] if your case isn't crystal-clear, and you wander and wait there until something tips the scales hopefully in your favor, like lots and lots of people back on Earth praying for you, or holding a mass for you, putting in enough good words and energy for you until St. Peter relents and lets you into heaven. So here is where a lifetime of practice at waiting in line would come in handy. Remember that next time you are at Safeway....

Judaism:
"(B)ecause Judaism is primarily focused on life here and now rather than on the afterlife, Judaism does not have much dogma about the afterlife, and leaves a great deal of room for personal opinion."[6]
"It is impossible to affirm that there is a good God while denying that there is any ultimate reward and punishment. If there is a just God, there is ultimate justice. Conversely, if there is no ultimate justice, there is no just God—which is the same as saying there is no God (if anything, belief in an unjust god is even bleaker than belief in no god)."[7]

Like my dentist tells me, "Deliberate too long about your problem teeth and your problems will all go away."
Creativity can't be solved by logic.

And yes, Virginia, there is a Santa Claus.

Islam:
As far as I can tell there is a Paradise here too, but it usually seems reserved for people who strap a bomb to themselves and blow it up with lots of other people around, providing of course those other people don't believe the same as you. And then you land in a wonderful place filled with lots of virgins, although when you don't have a physical body any more I'm not sure what good this is. This would sound to me actually more like a version of hell some jokes tell about.

On the positive side, and to avert someone declaring a holy war on me, I read that one's access to *Jannah*, or Heaven, is thought by more informed sources to be directly related to the good deeds you do in this life, not only to people but also to bugs and trees. And we could all learn from that.[8]

Buddhism:
Here there are many flavors of afterlife, in many of which there is no heaven at all. Instead, what you do here and now is important because you live forever anyway, and so why waste your time doing bad things which someone else will just do back to you later? (So the boomerang was invented by Buddha?)

Other versions of Buddhism don't waste their time theorizing about later; to them the present moment is the most important one, so if you sit and fantasize about a life hereafter you just waste precious here-and-now time not doing something here and now.[9]

For Tibetan Buddhists, life is a cycle of many lifetimes one after the other, until you've gotten rid of all the bad things in you and can graduate from this plane. Even more virtuous however is to voluntarily return to earth to teach other people, till all of us can graduate from this plane at once.

Hinduism:[10]
Here the belief prevails that your consciousness lives forever, so if you don't get it right this time you can try again next time. The twist here is that this can lead to the utter inertia of Couchpotatoitis--the down side of the adage "nothing ventured, nothing gained"—which in itself is a terrible malady, leading to twenty lifetimes as a cleaning lady while you hold back doing anything till you can get it right the first time. Or if you don't watch out you may come back as the beetle that your widow squashes in disgust, so you'd better get it right this time! For a light treatment of this topic, try the novel *Bad Karma*, by David Safier.

Atheism:
Here there is no afterlife, unless someone confuses it with half-life, as in the uranium which lives on infinitely longer in a hole somewhere than do humans, who are so much more evolved and entertaining than a nuclear waste dump. For the atheist, when you die, you are dead. Period. So for the atheist the radiance of uranium lasts longer than the radiance of my memory of my love's smile....

I rest my case.

American Indian: there are so many different flavors of Native American belief that this book will not try to do them justice. And some groups, like the Navajos, are pretty cagey anyway about what they really do believe; they have often been known to give outsiders different versions of their beliefs, all slightly augmented or fabricated out of true, to protect the integrity of the energy of their cosmos, so to speak.

Navajos I knew on the reservation when I lived there in the '80s who were of traditional belief felt it important to knock out a wall of the hogan where someone had died, to let out the spirit. Only certain same-sex family members were supposed to prepare the body for burial. Any contact with the dead required that one be cleansed afterward by a ceremony with the medicine man or woman. There is interestingly no word for "dead" in Navajo that I ever heard of; rather, the person who has died is simply "gone", and one is not supposed to talk about him anymore.

Aborigine:
"Death is the destruction of the body but not the spirit, this returns to its source. Like the totemic beings, it is indestructible. Even though in the Dreamtime stories they were sometimes 'killed' or 'died', their spirits remained part of the Eternal Dreaming stream, which included human beings."[11]

Like physics says, energy just changes form.

Funerals
An interesting article about funerals, however with a dearth of references, is the following:
 http://en.wikipedia.org/wiki/Funeral .

A variation on the funeral theme that I like is the Irish wake, in which people tell stories about the person who has passed on. A song by the Dubliners and others called "Finnegan's Wake" describes a wake that didn't end as expected. (Lyrics at: http://www.azlyrics.com/lyrics/dropkickmurphys/finneganswaketraditional.html)

Is all this useful? As information, yes; some of these cultures have centuries of experience with their models of dying. But these are also mostly cultures that are very different from ours; when I read in the Tibetan book of the dead about their gods and demons, I can't really find affinity with this, any more than when I read so avidly about their cosmology and saints in my 20s but still couldn't see myself going to Tibetan heaven.

One picture I get when perusing many of these versions of life after death is that they will serve for some folks as a deterrent against living a lazy, evil life this time, like grown-up versions of be good or the wolf will eat you up, or if not that the wicked witch will bake you for dinner. It's no wonder to me that people leave the church in droves, feeling like they are being talked down to. So in the U.S. people if anything tend to go off looking for or inventing their own religion, while here in Germany people mostly just leave the church and place their belief in the society as a whole and try to embody their beliefs along humanistic lines of "you be nice to me and I'll be nice to you". Here eternal life exists only in other people's memories of you; the body stays in the cemetery until relatives stop paying rent for the plot. So above all be good to your relatives, of course.

Notes

[1] The Fifth Ecumenical Council, Second Council of Constantinople: http://reluctant-messenger.com/origen7.html

[2] christianity.about.com/od/whatdoesthebiblesay/a/Hell-In-The-Bible.htm

[3] https://bible.org/article/what-bible-says-about-hell

[4] http://christianity.about.com/od/whatdoesthebiblesay/a/deathandheaven.htm

[5] http://en.wikipedia.org/wiki/Purgatory

[6] http://www.jewfaq.org/olamhaba.htm

[7] http://www.jewishjournal.com/dennis_prager/article/is_there_a_heaven_and_a_hell_20120615

[8] http://en.wikipedia.org/wiki/Afterlife#Ahmadiyya

[9] http://en.wikipedia.org/wiki/Buddhism

[10] http://en.wikipedia.org/wiki/Hinduism

[11] austhrutime.com/afterlife.htm

2. What the Research Says

Near Death Experiences

An immense amount of research has occurred in recent years on "near-death experiences", which bears attention in these pages.

So-called NDEs have occurred to people in situations where the body is subjected to trauma, for instance during a surgical procedure or a car accident. The person suddenly experiences their world as if outside the physical body, usually up near the ceiling, and can see their body inert below them; they can afterwards often relate just what was said by the people operating on them or otherwise attending to them. Sometimes something like a tunnel of light opens up; sometimes they speak with departed loved ones; sometimes they speak with a large and infinitely loving Someone whose identity may depend on the person's own belief system. For various given reasons the person returns to the body, and we the fortunate incarnate learn about their experiences, if they dare to talk about them.[12]

An astounding number of these tales have the above and other similar facets in common; it is unlikely that they all compared notes so they could tell the same story.

One of the pioneers in psychooncology, Elizabeth Kübler-Ross, eventually developed a very strong conviction that these stories were true experiences rather than hallucinations. (See References, *The Tunnel and the Light*)

Then there was that man named Robert Monroe, who wrote books after he found that he could leave his body at will. He systematically explored many different channels of consciousness, including where people go when they die.

He found first a place he referred to as "The Park", a sort of welcoming station where everybody lands to get their bearings. They are met by a greeter, and helped to get settled in. Many apparently take up activities similar to those in the life just finished, as a way to complete unfinished business.

Mr. Monroe himself has since departed for the final frontier; the group he founded to explore his work offers classes, recordings, and various possibilities for enlarging one's own worldview. See References for more information.

Professor Ian Stevenson, of the University of Virginia[13], conducted research with children in India and Europe who claimed to have memories of a life just ended, and who were often able to take him directly to where the person had lived, in a village far away where they had never been in this life.[14]

Notes

[12] http://en.wikipedia.org/wiki/Near-death_experience

[13] http://en.wikipedia.org/wiki/Ian_Stevenson

[14] http://en.wikipedia.org/wiki/Twenty_Cases_Suggestive_of_Reincarnation

3. Smoke This

Your death: what flavor could it have? Deliberate, or accidental? Sudden, or excruciatingly drawn out? With friends and loved ones, or alone among strangers, or alone on a mountain?

Sit somewhere quiet so you can have a reverie about a death and an afterlife of your choice. Sitting is usually better than lying, so you don't fall asleep. Try out different ones; be creative. For scary vision quests, however, it can be good to have someone you trust with you to anchor you while they sit nearby. Appropriately trained hypnotherapists would be my first choice if the trip gets too scary. Or your favorite medicine man.

Otherwise, if you decide to go it alone, be in a comfortable position and envision a safe place, your power place, from which you can go on vision trips. If you have never created one before, take first all the time you need to make one—at a seaside, for instance, or on a mountain; a favorite of mine finds me cosily inside a gigantic old tree. Furnish it as you like; make it nice and comfy—a place you like to go, a place where you feel safe.

Then sit there and look at your ideas and fears about death. What has brought you to this threshold? Are you in pain, or otherwise uncomfortable? If so, take care of that first. Is the body sick, or old, or injured? What unfinished business do you have? Look at your issues. Look at this life you are wearing, and all its challenges. Take your time; this is an important juncture, a flirt with your precipice from a safe place. Give it all the attention it needs. Notice that you-the-witness are separate from your experiences. Notice that. Walk among them and through them like through a department store looking at all your garments. Keep a journal if you like.

Is death scary? What scares you the most? Face your monster at the gate. Explore all his facets one by one if you are really courageous or crazy: death by drowning, falling, gunshot, heart attack, broken heart, broken legs, cancer, drugs, ...and the list goes on and on, one flavor for every girl and boy, one lid for every saucepan.

Remember that you are watching all this from a safe place. You can take the tour without falling into the witch's cauldron just yet.

What flavor does your monster have? Savor him, then eat him. Yes, you read right—eat him. Don't spit him out. Digest him, and let him come out the normal way. Because if you don't eat him, he will definitely continue to eat you. First your toes, then your ears...like the giant chocolate Easter bunny I got when I was little.

From your sanctuary place have a look at what hopes or fears hold you to the earth. Some people become monks in order to do this, and spend the rest of their lives exploring their hopes and fears and facing them so they can let them go, so as to reach the gates of Heaven as light and unencumbered as little children, or like Socrates so light that they can rise like a feather into the higher realms.

Other people prefer a balance of doing vs. contemplating, or doing vs. complicating. And still others have the luxury of not being able to get out of bed any more, and have time to explore fully their inner realms, where no one has gone before.

This kind of exploration can have the purpose of resolving issues binding up your energy, or can itself become a binding energy which feeds on itself forever. So find some happy middle ground, okay? In the References at the end of this book are sources which explore further avenues.

4. Roll Your Own

What's the answer? Who is right? What is the Truth? Here the best information I have is: Find or invent your own. A tenet of meditation is that your own answers lie within. That sounds like a cheap cop-out for someone used to opening a book or a laptop and finding the answers there; but when the answers depend on who I am and what makes me tick, then it starts to make sense: what answer is right to me depends on what language I speak, what culture I have, what time I live in—in other words, what preconceptions I have about the way the world around me works.

So Heaven is like homeopathy: what works for some won't work for others. That's why there are so many religions, so that there is a flavor for everyone. There's even a religion for people without religion. AND looking within means you don't have to buy a computer first or borrow one to get your answers. That means No Excuses Apply. "No matter where you go, there you are."

How to find my own answers?

Sit there and wait. No, don't go to Helen Waite.

Sit there and wait? Exactly what you learn all your life NOT to do, right? But try it, you'll like it. After you go through a few layers of gunk around your mind that you've picked up along the way telling you what and who you are and that you MUST absolutely

NOW do such and such, maybe you start to notice that you aren't your experiences; you just carry them around for entertainment. And if your own experiences aren't enough for you, you can turn on a hundred channels of Reality TV and watch other people's lives as they happen—or seem to. Or turn to Reality News a la CNN, and watch the latest Trayvon Martin show blow by blow. Of course, now we don't need to do that anymore either—we now have smartphones as a new attention magnet on top of all the others, so we can twitter and tweet our way to perfect digital connectedness, just barely avoiding the telephone pole in our paths because the smartphone screen is SO interesting. And in a not distant tomorrow near you we'll no doubt be able to just sit at home like Bruce Willis in *Surrogates* and let our avatars live life for us.

Behold the onion; what will she look like when she's peeled? Are you game to find out? Don't be so sure. You might not like the way you look when you're naked. What if there were actually something still there when all the layers of the onion were peeled away?...That might be the you left over when you're dead. Take a deep breath.

So how do I sit there and wait? There must be a right way to do this. So then be "proactive", go and buy a book, find a barefoot teacher speaking and doing bizarre things in the mountains of Mexico, India, Santa Fe, or East Poughkeepsie. Whatever bakes your cookie. Go have fun. And then come back and wait. And do what? There must be something to do while I'm waiting.

Sure there is. Occupy the mind while you're waiting, if you'd like—give it something to do so it doesn't drive you crazy while you wait for the bus. Sit and envision bright colors and energy streams, if you want, like in Amy Wallace's *The Psychic Healing Book*. Pray to saints or talk to them if you want to, or punish yourself in the manner of your choosing if it makes you feel better or tames your demons. And then go back and watch the show. Eventually it will stop—or at least so they say. Curtain call.

And then what?

So when it stops, you get on the bus. That's what bus stops are for. But don't forget your umbrella—you may meet the love of your life there in the rain. And don't forget your towel.

5. Bus Stops and Umbrellas

But do I want it to stop? What happens next? That sounds like death. What's it like after I die? Is there anything after I die? (What if there isn't?)

Having viewed numerous of my own past lives, I still don't have an answer about the between time. I don't remember the time in between lives. For me the stages of death and dying that work for Tibetans don't work so well, but I can respond to the notion found in various schools of thought of my consciousness having its body in different layers, like an emotional one, a mental one, and so on right on out to the physical body, and it makes sense to me that they would have to drop off one by one as I leave my body and this lifetime behind—like the snake shedding its skins. (Oh, you don't like snakes? Well—oops.)

As with many Americans, I have moved to a new town more often in my life than I usually care to think about; each time I leave behind what I don't need any more. —And usually buy a new one again at the next Wal-Mart, but that destroys the nice simile, doesn't it? Or not.

As I mentioned in Chapter 2, Robert Monroe (no, not Roger Moore, but maybe Raymond Moody), in his books about his *Journeys Out of the Body (see References)*, describes his own exploration of places people go to right after they die—places where they can orient themselves to their new circumstances. A designated greeter meets people to help them get settled in. (So that is where Wal-Mart greeters go next....) New arrivals often start by recreating surroundings and activities like those they knew during physical life, to make getting used to not being physical easier by doing it step by step, and also in order to finish things they were not finished with doing yet. It reminds me of the 1998 Robin Williams film, *What Dreams May Come.*

6. Body Dynamics

Being nobody
Is death and dying scary? You bet it is—for the body, at least. The unknown is scary as hell. Body knows only here and now, and it's scared to death to feel that it is about to stop existing. (Thank you Lewis Bostwick, wherever you are.) On the other hand: what if you-the-consciousness doesn't stop existing?

So if you don't die when you die—what then? It's still scary to think of dying—after all, there are no travel guides at Barnes and Noble between Croatia and Estonia that cover Dying. What happens when you are forced to leave all that you hold near and dear behind you forever? That's a long time. And such a pity to leave behind that island refuge in Bermuda...

EXERCISE
Go to your sanctuary. Gets easier each time, doesn't it? Now think of the people that you have unfinished issues with. Go through your list, and see with each person what unfinished business you have. It could just be that you didn't tell them you cared about them often enough, or you can't bear the thought of leaving them after promising to always provide for them in life. Go down your list then and do and say all those things you want to. Today is always a good place to start; who knows if you have another one coming?

EXERCISE
Now look at the unfinished business you have with...yourself. What dreams have you had that will never get realized now? Where were you not strict enough on yourself, or too strict? Who didn't you please enough? Who did you please and thereby leave out your own needs? Spend some time with each place where your energy hangs up; make a list here too if it helps. Play out alternative endings that go out the way you would have liked them to.

Then put all the judgments about yourself into a box, wrap them up as a beautiful gift, and put them in a chute to whisk away to God, or whatever you call her/him. Be aware that really you've done as well as you could at the time. And now the time is up with regrets, the buzzer sounds ZZZZZZZZZZZZZZT, and no more time for self pity. Wastes energy in the time you have left. Starting now, live each moment as if it were your last. Hell, it just might be your last. Try a new tack instead of regret: What will you do with today when it is your last day on the planet? But don't waste time telling me, dammit, just do it.

Aging

When people get old, the aging process is a good exercise in letting go, isn't it? It's kind of like dying in increments. When two of my back teeth had to be taken out a few years ago because they couldn't be fixed any more, that felt like my known world was coming to an end. My reaction amazed me. It took a while beforehand to get used to the idea that the two husks left of my two back teeth weren't going to be there anymore, even though they were long dead, and it was like part of me died when they came out. It sounds laughable to me now, but it's true.

So I can hardly imagine what it must feel like to lose a whole organ, or limb of my body. Or the whole body. Especially one piece at a time. Good God, I'm attached to it. Just seeing my face get older and older every year is a trip I would really rather not have to take. I see a person in the mirror who doesn't look like me any more—all wrinkles, no hair, and each year it gets worse. I can better understand my father-in-law now when he refuses to wear his hearing aids so we don't have to holler, or use his cane to get around. Hell, I'm not an old man; I just look like one.

So how can all that compare to the prospect of losing everything in the universe that you know and love? How in God's name can one prepare for that, if losing a tooth is such a monumental thing? What to do?

You could practice imagining what it might feel like to die, to discharge some of the fear and loathing. In one of my lifetimes I died of drowning; when I re-experience that or anything whatsoever in that direction it gives me the creeps and I get panicky, but since I don't like swimming or being in water where I can't feel the earth under me anyway it's a good therapy. But I still avoid swimming in deep water. I don't want sharks nibbling on my toes, that's all.

Another time I died on some battlefield somewhere, killed by something I didn't even see coming; so I go back there in thought to bask in the splendid hopelessness of feeling my life ooze away. Another time I sentenced women to be burned alive as witches; later one of my victims became my girlfriend, so when I realized this I saw things through her eyes, and had to face up to what part of me had done. Yes—that's reincarnation therapy, very big in Holland. I suppose their health insurance will even pay for it; they seem open to trying many things if they show promise.

"Time flies like an arrow;
Fruit flies like a banana."

—Groucho Marx

Intermezzo

Here's an exercise in colors, pictures, music, smells, tastes, sensations—a trip in free association, just to see what comes up. Like LSD without the LSD.

At the outset you may either have a specific question in mind, or just let the most pressing matter your subconscious may have come up without your having to choose it or filter it. Start with your eyes closed. Go to your power place, and begin to just let thoughts go by, like on that big TV screen you always or never wanted to have: let everything go by that occupies you at the moment, or just make something up—but don't dwell on anything, just let it go by, one thought after the other. When each one that passes cries out for attention, wants you to stop the bus and occupy yourself with it, just greet it, tell it you will come back to it when the bus comes back, and drive on; sit back and enjoy the show—but with a twist:

Try this trip using any of your five or however many senses you want to have. You could change the channel so that all the information that vies for your attention is turned into colors, or sounds, or tastes, or sensations. Make for instance a symphony out of your life, and surf through its fugues and crescendos, splashing and crashing with its storms, or lilting gently on the summer's day of blissful peace. Squeeze yourself through terrifying narrowness of a birth canal, or teeter on a black abyss without a safety net in sight. Let sensations and impressions wash through and over you. When they make sense, that's fine—glean the sense from them, and be thankful for new insights. If they don't, just postulate that they do make sense to some level of you, and let the information reach the intended part of you without trying to process it through logic or other faculty for which the information isn't made anyway. If little slugs or crabbies want to fasten to you, notice that when you stop fighting them they can simply slip off your skin as you continue your journey.

When you come back, look at all the seashells you've found. Breathe, and return completely to your body...Chunk. Let a golden sun of energy come in and replenish you. Welcome back.

8. More Body Dynamics

Having a body is such a great thing. It makes the world so simple. Everything revolves around what the body needs sometimes—feed me, wash me, let me sleep, let me make love...

The world is simple in the body; the world is clear. When you put down your glasses in one room, they will be there when you come back to them later—unless of course your wife puts them away for you in the meantime. When you buy beautiful clothes and put them in a closet to wait for you till you wear them, you know they will be there when you want to get them out again.

It's easy to forget that we are just the driver of this vehicle called the body; we easily forget that—it is not us.

The next exercise is not for the faint-hearted. This may be the scariest part of this whole book. This exercise is about imagining that you don't have a body any more.

Take some deep breaths after reading that, and notice if your pulse is racing as the body goes into fear. That's okay if it is; that's a normal body reaction.

Think about the world you visit when you dream. You may notice that things change very easily from one thing to another, and scenes change from one into another without your having to go anywhere. A clock can melt through your fingers *à la* Salvador Dalí. A person with you is someone that you know is your spouse, although it doesn't look like them at all. A tree may rise up on legs to chase you. You might walk up to a lounging albino tiger and pet it, because hell, you can't run away now anyway—and it doesn't jump up and eat you, but purrs instead.

A nice thing about having a body is that the thoughts around us which have created physicality vibrate so slowly that they pretty much stay put and act like physical objects. It's usually considered impossible to make them take another form, or if they can they have to go through established steps and behave pretty much the same each time. Most everybody on the planet has been taught in childhood to learn to see and interact with the world in just a certain way, so that they get results that are comparable to those everybody else gets. When you meet someone from a different culture, however, it takes a while to understand the filters and rules they know about this physical world that are different from yours; sometimes that seems fascinating and exciting, and sometimes that can be a real pain because you know the sky is blue and they know the sky is green and communicating with them is simply too frustrating to seem worthwhile. (And so people go to war until everyone left alive decides the sky is green...)

EXERCISE: being no body
So relax, and go to your sanctuary. Center yourself both in your head, and in your heart. Do that by first pulling your awareness of self into your head; then be aware also of your heart, the center of feeling and connectedness. Notice how the heart connects you to all things, and people, and times, and places. Enjoy this moment for as long as you please. Let the heart bask in its own sunshine.

Be in that place of safety and refuge, which you can go to whenever you want. That place exists whether you have a body or not. Hmm, maybe it could be a place to go to as you die. I might try that one unless I come up with something better.

So then populate your refuge with your "power objects". To do that, reflect on what gives you power, whether it's an object, or a photo, or a memory, and bring together symbols that remind you of these things. If you want you can reproduce these power objects in the physical world too, like shamen do to help them focus and channel their healing abilities. And above all, enjoy yourself! No one comes out of this alive! Or do they?

Look down at your imaginary body. What are you wearing? Now change the color of what you have on. Change it two or three times, and settle on colors you like.

Try out what it's like to fly. Let yourself rise up, up and see what your world looks like from above. Fly in closer to something and have a look at it. Come down and land. Walk up to a wall somewhere, and just gently nonchalantly...walk through it. Sit down in a chair, look at a table, and imagine a cat just appearing to sit on it. Observe her for a moment. Stand your mental body up, pet the cat, and then will yourself back to your sanctuary. Just like that. And then at your own pace, come back into your physical body. Button your physical and astral chakras in together if you like, like a zipper. Take some deep breaths, wiggle fingers and toes. Don't forget the gold sun of recharging energy. Open your eyes.

Amazing—you've just survived a trip without your body. Good job. Easier than you expected, wasn't it?

Okay. Let's go a step further. What if one day you wake up dead—and the bus doesn't come? No one comes to pick you up, no archangels and heavenly choirs to take you to your assigned cloud. What then? We've got to cover all eventualities. What if you don't have a body any more, but you are still walking around in the world you just left? No one can hear you, no one can see you. Your world goes on around you, but you're just not there. Put that feeling on; bask in its hopelessness, its frustration. Do this as long as you want. If you've gotten this far as a dead person though then there must surely be a next stop on the bus; no energy goes lost in this universe, and you are one of the most precious examples of energy that there is. So somebody must know where you are. Explore where you are, and process. Then when you are ready, come back to the physical body, zip yourself in, and take a deep breath. Center yourself back in your head and your heart; this is the place where you are in control of your world. Notice where in your body the fear of this experience sits, and move some of it out with your hands, or whatever method suits you. Let it go if you can. Let the charge of this experience flow right out of you and into the earth: spiritual compost. Here is about the time when lots of people begin to believe in God, to fill in that empty place. If you are sitting there in that empty place right now, well congratulations. Welcome to life. Smile, and wait for your bus to come—or just read that old copy of *People* magazine over there on the bench.

Let this place where you are mutate to your power place, and wait. Yes, you read right—your power place is wherever you are right now, centered in your head and your heart. Bring in a golden sun of purest you energy to charge you back up. Oh, you just went through an exercise and I didn't even announce it. Oops.

9. The Final Answer

Is there miracle healing? My answer: Don't come to me for answers. Find your own, dammit. I personally knew people who went to the knifeless surgeons in Brazil; they experienced firsthand how the healers reached inside their bodies and fished around to pull out sick energy. It happened to them and I believe them; otherwise I would never have believed that that was possible. Whether you do is up to you.

Once I accidentally pinched a girl from across the room without physically touching her. I know that happened, because I saw the sudden astonishment in her face when I imagined it, in the same moment as her hand went to her bottom, exactly to the place I imagined. So I am convinced that impossible things can happen. But you go find your own answers. If you don't, they may find you.

If you or someone you know has a terminal illness, whether or not that can be taken out of the body is beyond the scope of this book. Its purpose is to give the dying who are living—and that includes all who read this—things to think about, and exercises to practice to get to know themselves better. So if I raise more questions than I answer, that's good. My essay will be a springing board to your further assays into the unknown.

10. Finis

Is there life after death? Which came first, the chicken or the egg? Or are they the same thing in different continuums? Yes, I agree, that's trite. And true.

So here is your last exercise: a poem from e. e. cummings, one of my favorite poets. I can give it different interpretations, depending on my mood.

"o purple finch
              please tell me why
this summer world(and you and i
who love so much to live)
                        must die"

"if i
    should tell you anything"
that eagerly sweet carolling
self answers me)
                "i could not sing"

☙

ABOUT THE AUTHOR

I am on the sunny side of 60 (and which side is that? you may ask), and have experience in various directions, including registered nurse (30 years), taxi driver, waiter, lay pastor, meditation teacher, dock worker, artists' model. I married the same beautiful woman twice; I live with her in Hamburg, Germany. My first contact with death outside my family—besides the bugs that I blew to smithereens with firecrackers when I was a kid—came in my work in home health care in 1999. So many people out there tapping their white canes into the void...and it is a privilege to be allowed to accompany them.

References and Further Reading

Dispenza, Joe, D.C. (2012). *Breaking the Habit of Being Yourself: How to Lose Your Mind and Create a New One.* Retrieved from www.amazon.com. Kindle Edition.

Ighisan, Mircea. (2012). *WOW! How to create new realities.* Retrieved from www.amazon.com. Kindle Edition.

Kübler-Ross, Elisabeth. (2012). *The Tunnel and the Light: Essential Insights on Living and Dying.* Retrieved from www.amazon.com. Kindle Edition.

Monroe, Robert. (1992). *Journeys Out of the Body.* New York, NY: Three Rivers Press.

Safier, David. (2013). *Bad Karma.* Oxford, UK: John Beaufoy Publishing.

Stevenson, Ian. (2003). *European Cases of the Reincarnation Type.* Jefferson, NC: McFarland and Company.

—. (1966). *Twenty Cases Suggestive of Reincarnation.* Charlottesville, VA: University Press of Virginia.

Wallace, Amy. (1981). *The Psychic Healing Book.* Berkeley, CA: Wingbow Press.

Dying in Other Cultures

Tibet: http://www2.lib.virginia.edu/exhibits/dead/index2.html

Ancient Egypt: http://en.wikipedia.org/wiki/Book_of_the_Dead

Weltreligionen (German): http://www.leben-tod.de/leben_nach_dem_tod.html

NDEs (Near Death Experiences)

Near Death Experience: http://en.wikipedia.org/wiki/Near-death_experience

Near Death Experience Research Foundation: http://www.nderf.org/religion_spirituality.htm

Elisabeth Kübler-Ross Model: http://en.wikipedia.org/wiki/K%C3%BCbler-Ross_model

Elisabeth Kübler-Ross Foundation: http://www.ekrfoundation.org/

Robert Monroe: http://www.monroeinstitute.org

☙